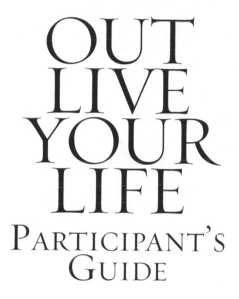

OUT LIVE YOUR LIFE

PARTICIPANT'S GUIDE

OUT LIVE YOUR LIFE

PARTICIPANT'S GUIDE

Based on the DVD featuring *New York Times* Best-Selling Author

MAX LUCADO
PREPARED BY DAVID DRURY

THOMAS NELSON
Since 1798

NASHVILLE   DALLAS   MEXICO CITY   RIO DE JANEIRO

Published in Nashville, Tennessee, by Thomas Nelson. Thomas Nelson is a registered trademark of Thomas Nelson, Inc.

The publishers are grateful to David Drury for his writing assistance and collaboration in developing the content for this guide.

Thomas Nelson, Inc., titles may be purchased in bulk for educational, business, fund-raising, or sales promotional use. For information, please e-mail SpecialMarkets@ThomasNelson.com.

Unless otherwise noted, Scripture quotations are taken from THE NEW KING JAMES VERSION. © 1982 by Thomas Nelson, Inc. Used by permission. All rights reserved.

Scripture quotations marked MSG are from *The Message* by Eugene H. Peterson. © 1993, 1994, 1995, 1996, 2000. Used by permission of NavPress Publishing Group. All rights reserved.

Scripture quotations marked NCV are from the New Century Version®. © 2005 by Thomas Nelson, Inc. Used by permission. All rights reserved.

Scripture quotations marked NIV are taken from the HOLY BIBLE: NEW INTERNATIONAL VERSION®. © 1973, 1978, 1984 by International Bible Society. Used by permission of Zondervan Publishing House. All rights reserved.

Scripture quotations marked NLT are from the *Holy Bible*, New Living Translation. © 1996. Used by permission of Tyndale House Publishers, Inc., Wheaton, Illinois 60189. All rights reserved.

ISBN: 978-1-4185-4395-2

Printed in the United States of America

10 11 12 13 14 WC 5 4 3 2 1

For the Christian, none is higher than this: when we love those in need, we are loving Jesus. It is a mystery beyond science, a truth beyond statistics. But it is a message that Jesus made crystal clear: when we love them, we love him.

—Max Lucado

CONTENTS

INTRODUCTION

You've been given an honest-to-goodness human life, complete with summers and songs and ice cream and tears. You didn't ask for it, but you have it. Now what are you going to do with it? What if you rocked the world with hope? Infiltrated the four corners of the earth with God's love and life?

What if you followed the example of the very first church in Jerusalem? This tiny sect expanded their impact to become a world-changing force. How did they do it? What can we learn from their priorities and passion? Let's ponder their stories, found in the first twelve chapters of Acts. Let's examine each event through the lens of this prayer: "Do it again, Jesus. Do it again."

God has given this generation, *our generation*, everything we need to alter the course of human suffering. He invites us to outlive our lives, not just in heaven but here on earth. Are you ready to live in such a way that your death is just the beginning of your life?

How This Study Works

There are four weeks to this study, and each week includes five readings—days one through five. You'll do this part of the study alone, and you will want to have a Bible and pen in hand. Every reading includes an "Act like Acts" section, which challenges you to follow the example of the earliest Christians, and an "A Life Outlived" reflection and question for you to ponder throughout the day.

You will find a few special sections spread throughout the pages as well. "Get Unshelled" offers an opportunity to reflect on the parts of your life that close you off to the world and to consider ways to break out of your shell. "A Mile in Their Shoes" gives creative and relatively simple ways for you to experience firsthand the needs of others, to grow your compassion for their situations. Finally, each week includes a "Legacy Starter" that presents an ambitious idea for you to consider. Some of these may seem impossible at first, but with a group of people passionately working together, you'll be amazed at the legacy you can leave. Just like the early church in Acts, with the Holy Spirit giving you the power, the possibilities are limitless.

Throughout the guide, you will find blocks of text that have been placed in italics. These are quotes taken directly from *Outlive Your Life*.

Next, your group will gather to discuss the "Group Discussion" sections each week. There is a group activity to do before you watch the *Outlive Your Life* video. After you watch the video interviews and stories, you'll have time to discuss your thoughts on the subject matter.

Your group may be brand-new or have years of connection. Whatever the case, use this *Outlive Your Life* study to take things to the next level. Start by sharing from your heart on the issues raised. You may not think your group is large enough to make a difference. What could less than a dozen people do in a world so filled with tragedy, disease, and war? Well, Acts is exactly that kind of story. We already know that less than a dozen people made all the difference. Now it's your turn.

Here's a salute to a long life: goodness that outlives the grave, love that outlasts the final breath.

WEEK

MAKING
LIFE
COUNT

"But you will receive power
when the Holy Spirit comes
upon you. And you will be my
witnesses, telling people about
me everywhere—in Jerusalem,
throughout Judea, in Samaria,
and to the ends of the earth."

(Acts 1:8 NLT)

❀ Day 1: What He Left

The followers of Jesus Christ are countless, but he never founded an organization. No one knew more than he did, but he never wrote down his thoughts. No person experienced more pain, but he never inked a memoir telling us the details of how it felt. Jesus didn't leave behind what most anyone else might have. No buildings bearing his name, no trust funds to protect his wealth, no museum exhibits to display his earthly goods. There's no Fortune 500 company with high-rise headquarters in New York or Tokyo. So what was the legacy of Jesus Christ? What did he leave behind?

He left *them*. Jesus left fewer than a dozen disciples. People. People who loved him and were ready to do what he asked. People who loved and supported one another. People who loved God and loved each other enough to change the world: because that's what he left behind. He also left *us*. We are called into the ongoing story of what happened after Jesus ascended into heaven—a story that is still happening.

For the most part, we live normal lives. We sit in the bleachers, eat at diners, change diapers, and wear our favorite team's ball cap. We aren't famous and no one notices when we walk down the street. We're regular folk . . . just like the Jerusalem disciples. He used them to change the world. Could he use us too?

Yes. All the time. Because Acts is not just the story of *them*. It's the story of *us*.

There the disciples tell us the life-changing message of Jesus. They call us to affirm what they believe and to do the kinds of miraculous things they did.

Act like Acts

Read Acts 1:4–11.

■ It's not enough for us to do well. We want to do good. What has Jesus left for you to do for him? Can you name a specific thing you are already sure God wants you to do? What are you waiting for?

A Life Outlived

■ The apostles were regular folks—fishermen, tax accountants, prostitutes, and revolutionaries. They didn't have friends in high places, but they did have a fire in their bellies to change the world. When have you seen God use regular folks to make a difference?

Get Unshelled:
What You Believe

The book of Acts is full of moments in which the disciples came out of their shells. God brought them opportunities to share their faith. In chapter 2, Peter didn't pass up the chance to speak to the crowd who thought the believers were drunk. And when he and John were hauled into court in chapter 4, they took it as a chance to share the gospel, not their own legal defense. When Stephen was persecuted to the point of death, he still talked about what mattered most (chapter 7). When Philip hitched a ride with an eager Ethiopian, when a centurion called Peter, and when Ananias met the infamous and dangerous Saul, the same thing happened: the truth was shared. The early disciples did not keep their beliefs to themselves or hunker down in their shells. Instead, God unshelled them and gave them opportunities to express what they believed.

What do you believe? When opportunities come your way, how do you react? Or when the next turning-point question comes, how will you reply?

To explain what you believe, you don't need to use the fancy terminology someone else might use. Remember, after Peter and John spoke effectively of Jesus, their persecutors didn't "take note that they were really smart and impressive." No, instead they "realized that they were unschooled, ordinary men" and "took note that these men had been with Jesus" (Acts 4:13 NIV).

Answer the following questions to help you put what you believe into words.

■ *What is God like?* If someone who didn't know much about the Bible and was not a Christian asked you to describe what God is like, what would be your answer? What experiences do you have to show this? What scriptures could you point to that support your response?

■ *Why do you need God?* How would you tell your story of why you need God? What has God done in you that changed your life from what it was before? Or, what might your life be like if you didn't know God?

■ *What can God do through you?* What big thing is God doing in the world through believers like you? What grand plan is God up to that you could recruit people to join? If someone asked you what you think the church's mission should be, how would you respond?

🐾 Day 2: Face-to-Face

The numbers are devastating. Disease. Disaster. Death. So many people lost to preventable diseases or abandoned in the aftermath of AIDS. Earthquakes level shantytowns. Tsunamis wash away island nations. War leaves behind another wake of refugees. The statistics convict us as we see or hear of so many hurt and hungry. So many with so little. What can be done in face of it all?

Perhaps the greatest tragedy is when these problems remain distant. Only numbers, not names. Just facts, not faces. But when we take a good, long look into their eyes, instead of looking away, we move past the stats and stories and become a part of the solution.

"Make a careful exploration of who you are and the work you have been given, and then sink yourself into that" (Gal. 6:4 MSG). What's your language when it comes to serving others? Whether you communicate best with children, teenagers, drug addicts, executives, or the elderly, "God has given us different gifts for doing certain things well" (Rom. 12:6 NLT). God designed you this way for a reason.

You might get inspired and sponsor a child. You may dig wells. You could fund missionaries, staff hospitals, build schools, or launch churches. Maybe you befriend someone to whom you would not typically reach out. For at least one child, one family, one village, and maybe even an entire people group, you might be able to make a small but significant difference. Remember the scene at the end of *Schindler's List*? They engraved a Jewish proverb on the ring they gave their boss-turned-liberator: "Whoever saves one life saves the world entire."

> Our society is set up for isolation. We wear earbuds when we exercise. We communicate via e-mail and text messages. We enter and exit our houses with gates and garage-door openers. Our mantra: "I leave you alone. You leave me alone." Yet God wants his people to be an exception.
>
> **—Max Lucado**

Act like Acts

Read Acts 3:1–10.

■ What was asked for and what was given? You might be asking God for one thing but he would actually like to give you something much better. The same could be true for those in need around you. Consider some ways to give more than the bare minimum to others and to instead bless them with more than they asked for or imagined.

A Life Outlived

■ Notice who looked at whom first in verses 4–5 of Acts 3. Peter and John didn't fidget or turn away; they didn't get uncomfortable. Instead, they gave him an honest look. Why do you think this is an important part of the story?

■ The next time you see someone in need, be sure your kind eyes meet desperate ones. Will looking people in the eyes be hard for you? How might it make all the difference for them? For you?

✿ **Day 3:** What's in Your Hand?

In the Lord of the Rings movie *The Return of the King*, one of the key characters bears an interesting title. He is the "Steward of Gondor." This temporary steward's job is to use good judgment and take responsibility for the kingdom—to *steward* it—while the king of Gondor is away. What's more, when the true king returns, the steward is to return the throne to him.

The Bible speaks of this idea of stewardship. We often associate stewardship with the giving of money, and while it includes that, it is really so much more. A steward takes care of something that someone else owns, and while a steward may have control over how to use it, he must always remember who the real owner is. Consider what you have held in your hands in the last day. Have you held a steering wheel? A computer mouse? A wallet? A Bible? A friend's handshake? A phone? You are the steward of all those things.

We are the wealthiest Christians the world has ever known. We have technology and science on our side, helping us travel the world in a day or administer life-saving medicines with ease. We have all the resources we need to meet the needs of the day. From resources to relationships, you are the steward of all you touch and much of what you see every single day because someone else owns it all. The King. And he's coming back.

Act like Acts

Read Acts 4:32.

■ What thoughts come to mind as you read this passage? Try memorizing the verse this week. Write it on a card and post it on your mirror, in your office, or in your car. Repeat it often and try to recite it several times without looking. Hide it in your heart, and then live it out in your life.

A Life Outlived

God has given us everything we need to alter the course of human suffering in this world. The problem is not a lack of resources, but a need for workers, for people willing to give their time and energy to help a neighbor in need. In the face of all the needs you hear about, knowing where to start outliving your life is hard. But it begins with what you have in your hands every day. Make a list here of all the random things you have literally and figuratively had in your hand in the last twenty-four hours. How might God want you to use these resources more intentionally to steward them?

A Mile in Their Shoes:
Host a Poverty Meal

More than 13,000 children will die today because of hunger while Americans will spend almost 1 billion dollars eating out.[1]

What can you do about it? You can start by skipping the fast food or date night and instead host a Poverty Meal with your small group. It will provide a wonderful opportunity to spread the word about these needs and advocate for more action.

What Is a Poverty Meal?

A Poverty Meal is an opportunity to stand in solidarity with the hungry and speak out on their behalf. Those in attendance partake of the meal, usually a bowl of porridge or rice eaten while sitting on the floor to differentiate from the experience of a typical meal. The participants fast in preparation for the meal and then respond by donating what they *would* have spent eating out one meal. These funds help advocate for increased food assistance for the hungry. (Go to www.worldvisionacts.org/brokenbread for recipes, ingredients, and donation information. Or you may choose to partner with another anti-poverty program or humanitarian assistance organization instead.)

How Could We Really Do This?

☐ *Select a location.* Consider using a cafeteria, a dorm lunchroom, an outdoor pavilion, or a church fellowship hall. You'll need a stovetop to prepare the porridge and bowls to serve it in.

☐ *Gather resources.* World Vision provides free resources, including the authentic corn-soy-blend porridge mix that is often used in emergency situations worldwide, particularly in Africa. Provide water to drink.

☐ *Promote the event* in your church, neighborhood, workplace, or school for several weeks in advance. Partner with other organizations or groups that would want to participate.

☐ *Ask people to fast.* It is best for the participants to fast at least one meal earlier in the day to experience a more acute hunger than usual. Have only one intentionally inconvenient serving line.

☐ *Facilitate the hour.* During the meal you could play videos to build awareness, share prepared stories and statistics about the need, or open the floor to have people share about the needs with which they are familiar.

☐ *Help people respond.* Facilitate an intentional response at the Poverty Meal so they can donate the cost of one meal out and advocate for increased food assistance. Also, provide ways for people to talk about the experience at the event, whether in small groups as the whole crowd. Ask: How has this poverty meal changed your perspective, and how do you hope to adjust your priorities in the future?

✺ Day 4: One Body

Paul wrote 1 Corinthians as a letter to a church near Athens, Greece. In his letter, Paul told the Corinthians what church is all about. He didn't start where many of us would: with his preferences on worship styles or sermon topics. He didn't mention deacon boards or bulletin boards. Instead, Paul talked about the bigger picture of the church—a community with all things in common as the body of Christ.

The church is the body of Christ, made up of various people with various spiritual gifts. The problem comes when the parts of the body do not work together. Paul wrote of a hypothetical conversation between the different parts of the body, "If the foot should say, 'Because I am not a hand, I am not of the body,' is it therefore not of the body? And if the ear should say, 'Because I am not an eye, I am not of the body,' is it therefore not of the body?" (I Cor. 12:15–16).

Paul's explanation might sound ridiculous, but we clearly see how necessary the fingers, hands, and arms (and other "body parts") are in ministry. As members of the body of Christ, we are to be fully dependent on one another. We need one another's gifts and strengths. We cannot go it alone.

Can Democrats find common ground with Republicans? Can a Christian family carry on a civil friendship with the Muslim couple down the street? Can divergent people get along? The early church did—without the aid of sanctuaries, church buildings, clergy, or seminaries. They did so through the clearest of messages (the Cross) and the simplest of tools (the home).

—Max Lucado

Act like Acts

Read Acts 2:42–47.

■ Sharing is not just for kindergarten. It's a distinctive mark of Christian community, and Paul writes about it in this passage. This week, open up and tell someone something you normally wouldn't share. Let someone use your car or borrow your computer. Share your lunch or buy one for someone else. Build fellowship with other believers by having them into your home or going over to theirs. Have more "in common" with them by sharing what's yours. How could you reach out this week?

A Life Outlived

■ In Acts 2:42–47 we don't find any personal pronouns. It's not about us as individuals; it's about the body of Christ working together. We are more than unique followers of Christ; "We are parts of his body" (Eph. 5:30 NCV). "He is the head of the body, which is the church" (Col. 1:18 NCV). I am not his body; you are not his body. We—together—are his body. How does being a part of something bigger than you make outliving your life more possible?

✿ Day 5: The Main Thing

Have you ever gotten to your car and realized you had everything you needed for the day but the keys? Or maybe you have looked everywhere for your glasses and then finally found them . . . tucked in securely on top of your head. Missing what's important is frustrating. And sometimes what's important is right in front of us, but we don't see it because other things have gotten in the way and blurred our focus.

Even doing good things can distract us from the most important thing at times. Jim Collins, author of the wildly successful book *Good to Great*, reminded us: "Good is the enemy of great." It is certainly good for us to do all kinds of things to help those in need, to meet the physical challenges of poverty, hunger, and justice. However, if we do all the good things but miss out on offering them the one truly great thing we have—Jesus—perhaps it was all for naught.

Offering the salvation of Jesus without doing good works to serve people might be hypocritical, but offering good works without the salvation of Jesus is hollow.

Act like Acts

Read Acts 3:11–4:5.

■ In what environments do you have opportunities to share your faith? Who do you know with whom you could start a spiritual conversation that could make a difference in your life?

■ In the next seven days, pray that God would give you at least three such opportunities. When they come along, do as Peter did in Acts 3 and boldly share the good news of Christ's love and grace.

A Life Outlived

■ While secular aid organizations can give a bed, a meal, and valuable counsel, they don't feed the soul. But Christ gives so much more, and we can be the vessel for that message. We can give help for this life, but also hope for the next. Reflect throughout the day on the hope you have for the next life because of your faith in Jesus Christ. Who are some people who don't seem to have that hope in their hearts? Write their names below and pray for them frequently.

Legacy Starter:
Adopt-a-Country Project

If the American states were ranked as countries, eight of them would be in the top twenty-five economies in the world.[2] (Ontario, Canada, would also rank in the top twenty-five.[3]) As far as the rest of the States, thirty-eight of them would be in the top one hundred, and all fifty would be in the top two hundred if ranked independently.[4] Texas has a higher gross domestic product than all of India, and Illinois is far past Indonesia. Pennsylvania passes

Poland. New Jersey and North Carolina? Both are a few notches north of Norway. Thailand and Finland are behind Maryland. New York's economy hums larger than all of Australia. And catch this: California by itself would be the eighth largest economy in the world, more than the GDP of Spain, Brazil, or even Russia.

What could we do to make a difference for good with our larger slice of the pie? What could *you* do about it? One of the best ways to get involved is to combine efforts and sharpen your focus by adopting a country. Here's how:

☐ *Define the team.* Start by defining the group with whom you're working. This kind of legacy project is not one to tackle solo. If you have a larger extended family, see if you can pull them in to help. If you live in a dorm, get your whole floor in on it. Ask your entire church to be involved, or if you're in a large church, an entire ministry department. Your small group or Sunday school class would work. Your high school graduating class or even your neighborhood association might be options. Any previously defined group or community will do.

☐ *Take a Pulse.* After you have your team, take a pulse on the passions that already exist in the group. Perhaps several people have already visited a certain country in need. Or maybe a friend or relative is a missionary somewhere. A project on a smaller scale may have already been started that needs more emphasis. Whatever the case, it's not necessary to reinvent the wheel. Go where the passion is ignited, then stoke that spark into full flame.

☐ *Learn More.* Find out all you can about the needs in that
country. A prayer book entitled *Operation World* (Gabriel
Resources, 2001) is a valuable tool with information on
the needs in nearly every country's context and specific
ways to pray for that country. An interactive prayer map
is also found at http://operationworld. 24-7prayer.com/.
By researching online, visiting the library, or talking
to people who have visited that country, you and
your Adopt-a-Country Team can become prayer and
response experts on that country in no time.

☐ *Celebrate Short-Term Wins.* Start with a few projects you
can directly impact with your prayers and giving right
away. Most of these projects will have already started,
and you can join in what others are already doing. Team
up and make a difference right away.

☐ *Set Long-Term Goals.* As you become better informed
about the needs your adopted country has and the
resources your team brings, choose some strategic
problems to involve yourselves in over time. You might
sponsor the education of young women if your adopted
country restricts female education. Your group could
dig wells in a dry land or free trafficked children in a
corrupt city. You could help launch sustainable poor-
owned businesses, prevent the spread of AIDS, or fund
malaria medications. You might build a church, a school,
a fishery, or a farm. Whatever you choose to do, make
specific, attainable goals that you can come back to and
measure in one year, five years, and so on.

✸ **Group** Discussion

The puzzle is partially complete, but the picture isn't quite clear yet. You can make out something sort of yellow in the sky, some kind of building forming over on the left. People are in the foreground, but who knows how many. Over next to your half-completed puzzle are a bunch of pieces in irregular shapes and sizes. Every nub and notch is different. They might not look like much in a pile over there, but every one of them has a perfect fit as the puzzle is pieced together.

The same is true of the video today. You'll hear creative ways people have matched their interests, gifts, and connections with the deep needs in today's world. You might not see it coming . . . the puzzle pieces don't seem to fit anywhere at times. Then the perfect chance comes, the opportunity to make life count. It all fits together and the picture becomes clear.

The puzzle remains incomplete, however, without you and your group. Commit to the discussion after the video, helping each other discover where each person's puzzle pieces might fit.

1. Before you watch the video, ask each member of your group to write down their unique abilities, gifts, and resources. Put each item on a separate card or sticky note. Put everyone's cards or sticky notes up on the wall. Take a good, long look and then begin a conversation about your diverse assets. What might God ask you to do with your unique and diverse resources?

2. After you watch the video, discuss the following questions:

   a. What do you think of Shaun King and his efforts to raise money and awareness in innovative ways? What about his real-life story inspires you?

   b. When have you been exposed to great need in another place, like Tammy Whitaker was when she went to Africa?

c. What phrase or quote from the video most stood out to you? Which one do you think you'll remember the longest, and why?

3. Read Acts 2:1–21 aloud as a group. Build a list of all the descriptive words in this passage, words that help define who the disciples were and who the people hearing them were. Which of these words do you want to be true of your group?

4. What criticisms do you hear about past generations? Have you heard it said that certain groups of people should have done more in a particular situation (i.e., Christians should have done more to stop the Nazis in Germany during World War II)?

5. What criticism might future generations level against us when we are gone? When your grandchildren learn that you lived in a day in which 3 billion people were desperately poor and 1 billion people were hungry, what might they think of your response to the crises of your generation?

6. It is tempting to "forget the bread"—the core Gospel message—when you're serving others. What are some authentic ways to bring up the fact that Jesus not only meets our needs but also saves us from our sins?

7. Before you finish your meeting, take time to discuss the needs in which you find yourselves most "fluent." Who can you relate to best and what needs are you most passionate to meet? Fill out the following chart so you know the answers for your entire group (or use a separate sheet of paper).

Example:

Name: *Jane Doe*

Can relate to: *Single mothers*

Is passionate about: *Parenting children with learning disabilities*

Wants to make a difference by: *Perhaps doing something more in the school system*

Name:

Can relate to:

Is passionate about:

Wants to make a difference by:

"David had done the will of God
in his own generation . . ."

(Acts 13:36 NLT)

---

*Heavenly Father, I want to make a difference for you
in the world. I don't want future generations to look
back on my life and wonder why I did nothing to help.
Inspire my heart. Show me how to get involved in a
practical way, reveal to me opportunities to serve, and
give me the courage and dedication to pursue those
opportunities with passion. In Jesus' name I pray, amen.*

THE
POOR
AS PRIORITY

"The Spirit of the LORD is upon Me,
Because He has anointed Me
To preach the gospel to the poor;
He has sent Me to heal the brokenhearted,
To proclaim liberty to the captives
And recovery of sight to the blind,
To set at liberty those who are oppressed."

(Luke 4:18)

✿ Day 1: No Needy Persons

The earliest church in Jerusalem had many things to point to for proof that their new faith had truth and power. They could point to the revolutionary teachings of Jesus Christ. The crucifixion and resurrection were proof positive that Jesus was the atonement for sin— and that he was indeed God. Healing the sick, speaking in the language of foreigners, and prophesying about the future were all ways to show that this new Jewish movement was something of God.

The church in Acts grew and grew, but this growth was coupled with a very simple quality: having everything in common. These new followers of the risen Christ didn't treat their possessions the way everyone else did. Instead, they "shared everything they had" (Acts 4:32 NIV), and this sharing resulted in a community of Christ-followers who didn't have the typical layers of haves and have-nots. In fact, Acts 4:34 uses this astonishing description: "There were no needy persons among them" (NIV). It's not that they didn't show up needy. They often showed up because they had needs. In fact, those most in need were drawn to the early church: crippled beggars, widowed women, orphaned children, and freed slaves.

But because of their generous sharing, the early church had the best proof possible that their community was a truly transformative one: When a need arose, there was always enough to go around, enough to fill the need. Now that's a miracle!

Act like Acts

Read Acts 4:32–47.

■ What would it look like for you to share more of your stuff? One of the first things we teach children is to not be so possessive with their toys, to share with siblings or playmates. Perhaps one of the first things you can do is teach yourself to share what you have. Loan something valuable to a neighbor. Give money and don't track what is done with it. Have "everything in common" with your fellow believers at church. Look for an opportunity today to give away what you have and someone else needs.

A Life Outlived

■ Reflect today about God's view of the poor. Luke 4, Isaiah 61, and countless other scriptures make it clear that in God's economy the poor are to be loved. What does it say about the heart of our Father that he wants us to always be aware of those who have needs? What can you do to ensure you are never so far from the poor that you can't see them?

Get Unshelled:
Your Unmet Needs

We all have needs. Some needs are relational and emotional (friendship, community, love, peace, happiness, and contentment). We also have the intellectual need to learn or have certain questions answered. Other needs are more physical—food, water, clothing, and shelter. And spiritual needs include forgiveness, worship, and eternal life.

Consider which of these needs are being met and which are going unmet in your own life.

■ *Fulfilled Needs.* Which of your needs are best fulfilled? What relational, emotional, intellectual, physical, or spiritual needs are met for you on a consistent basis? Who or what meets these needs? Spend some time thanking God for your fulfilled needs.

■ *Unfulfilled Needs.* Which of your needs are least fulfilled? What relational, emotional, intellectual, physical, or spiritual needs are unmet for you on a consistent basis? Why are these needs unmet? Spend some time asking God to meet your needs—and for the grace to endure what unmet needs may continue in your life.

Now, turn the entire focus of this reflection around. *Consider the needs in the world today.* Think of a country for whose people you have a heart. Or consider a disadvantaged person you know or a part of your city that is ravaged by poverty. Which of their needs are being fulfilled or not being fulfilled? Think about each category mentioned above: emotional, relational, intellectual, physical, and spiritual. Ask for God's will in meeting their needs—and for God to empower you to find ways to help meet the needs of others.

✿ Day 2: Just Like Jesus

Healing the sick was a hallmark of Jesus' ministry. While he walked the earth, teaching parables and asking penetrating questions, he also healed people. Matthew 8:16 says that Jesus healed "all the sick" who were brought to him. But then he was crucified, rose again, and ascended into heaven. It seemed the window of opportunity had closed for those who needed healing.

However, in John 14:12 (NIV) Jesus made an interesting prediction: "I tell you the truth, anyone who has faith in me will do what I have been doing. He will do even greater things than these, because I am going to the Father." After the Holy Spirit came upon the disciples, Jesus' prediction happened exactly as he said it would. The previously inept disciples suddenly became healing experts. The sick and broken came in droves to be healed by the disciples, just as they had with Jesus. In Acts 5 we learn that people took the sick out into the streets on the mere possibility that the apostle Peter would walk by—hoping that perhaps his shadow would fall on them with healing power. In fact, as crowds of sick and disabled people gathered around the disciples, Acts 5:16 says, "*all* of them were healed" (NIV, emphasis added).

> It's no accident that *hospitality* and *hospital* come from the same Latin word, for they both lead to the same result: healing. When you open your door to someone, you are sending this message: "You matter to me and to God." You may think you are saying, "Come over for a visit." But what your guest hears is, "I'm worth the effort." Do you know people who need this message?
>
> **—Max Lucado**

Act like Acts

Read Acts 5:12–16.

■ The have-nots were a part of the earliest Christian community. Most scholars suggest that much of the early church was in fact made up of the lower classes and former slaves. What is the economic demographic of your church? Take steps this week to ensure your church is a welcoming place for the poor, sick, and disadvantaged. Think of ways to not only help those in need but also be a place that welcomes people who are poor and disabled into fellowship and worship. Find a way to make that invitation clear.

A Life Outlived

■ Poverty exposes the deep inequity in our world today. This should make you angry; it's just not fair. What would happen if you allowed righteous anger to cause you to get up and do something about it? How can you pray today for the poor in a simple way? How can you take action for the poor this week, a decision that will cost you something?

✿ Day 3: Who Gives You Orders?

It was a tense moment. The apostles were hauled into jail for preaching the gospel, but then an angel freed them from prison. The cops found these ex-cons back in the temple preaching the gospel again. By now the followers were growing; the faith of the apostles was rising even faster. Fearing the crowds, the prison guards kindly asked the apostles to come with them to the high court.

So the apostles found themselves back in front of the Jewish leaders of Jerusalem, the Sanhedrin court. Accusations flew. Threats were made. The leaders felt they were in an impossible situation. They didn't want to punish the apostles, but these men were preaching that they, as Jewish leaders, were partly responsible for murdering Jesus Christ and that in this new gospel Jesus was the Son of God. The chief priest reminded them: "Didn't we tell you never again to teach in this man's name?" (Acts 5:28 NLT).

The apostles couldn't deny the truth—the people in authority over them had given a direct order, and they had disobeyed. Not only that, but they had also escaped prison to do so. The apostles didn't quibble on that charge. Perhaps claiming that an angel let them go might have seemed like an insanity defense. However, the apostles cited a higher court than the Sanhedrin: "We must obey God rather than human authority" (Acts 5:29 NLT). When it comes to spiritual matters, the court of the Trinity has jurisdiction in this matter. The apostles had to follow God's orders, and how can you argue with that?

Act like Acts

Read Acts 5:27–32.

■ What are you doing to listen to God's orders? Instead of reading a book or watching television tonight, instead of entertaining yourself in some way to relax, spend thirty minutes in quiet with a notebook or sheet of paper on hand. Write down what God may be saying to you today.

A Life Outlived

■ During your time of reflection mentioned above, use the following questions to prompt your prayers and help you listen to God's commands for you:

1. Lord, what attitudes do I have that you want me to change?
2. Lord, what habits do I engage in that are a barrier in hearing from you?
3. Lord, what actions do you want me to take?

A Mile in Their Shoes:
Fasting

We often say that we are "hungry" or even thoughtlessly say, "I'm starving" if we miss a meal. In reality, few of us know what deep hunger really feels like, and after you've seen a picture of a starving person, it removes that word from your vocabulary pretty quickly. When your stomach grumbles or you "feel hungry," these sensations are only the first waves of hunger. Your stomach acid is just looking for more food to digest. Acute hunger, however, is felt in the mouth and throat, and its ramifications are severe. In fact, every second one person dies directly or indirectly from hunger.[5]

No doubt, we should be praying for this worldwide crisis. One of the most ancient and effective ways to pray is to fast—to deprive yourself of a meal or many meals in order to focus your mind and heart on prayer. Engage in the discipline of fasting in one of the following ways and direct your prayers for those around the world who do not have enough to eat.

☐ *Selective fast.* Give up a certain kind of food or categories of food (sweets, meat, etc.) for a season. This is a very common fast during the church season of Lent leading up to Easter.

☐ *Once-a-month fast.* Set aside a certain day each month to fast, such as the first Friday. On these days it is important to structure your day with a few times of intentional prayer.

☐ *Meal-of-the-week fast.* Pick a certain meal within each week to fast over a period of time, such as a month or six weeks. Perhaps you may want to fast during lunch every Wednesday, for example. Schedule this time to ensure you don't just work through the hour but instead spend that time in prayer.

☐ *One-meal-a-day fast.* For forty days or for Lent, some people will fast a certain meal every day or engage in a daytime fast where they don't eat at all while the sun is up, but eat breakfast or dinner when it's dark out.

☐ *Extended fast.* Whenever going without food for multiple days at a time, consult your physician first. Under the proper guidance of a doctor, a multiple-day fast in prayer can be a transformative and, intense experience.

🐾 Day 4: The Overlooked

The early church in Jerusalem started out on the right foot helping those in need. They welcomed all kinds of people into their ranks. However, an insidious problem developed right under the apostles' noses: neglect of widows due to racial favoritism.

In first-century culture, when a woman's husband died she had no way to support her family, so the Jerusalem church created a system to distribute food to widows in need. This distribution program in and of itself was a great step forward, and all was working well except for one thing. The Jews who administrated the program were favoring the

Jewish widows, leaving the Greek widows to suffer alone. Complaints started to come in. The food pantry program was playing favorites.

They called the first big meeting of the early church. This board meeting wasn't about theology or worship. It didn't involve a building or a parking lot. The first vote of the church ensured those people who were being overlooked would be served in the future. Isn't that significant? The neglected mattered enough to bring the entire church's attention to them.

As a solution, the best and brightest among them were chosen to spearhead the project; these men had a "good reputation" and were "full of the Holy Spirit and wisdom" (Acts 6:3). They didn't just have a clipboard and sign-up sheet in the lobby to handle this one. Instead, the church made it a priority and solved a problem that would have caused division and racial prejudice to corrupt the church's early days.

> The apostles were spiritual leaders. They fed souls, not stomachs. They dealt in matters of sin and salvation, not sandals and soup. Couldn't they dismiss the disparity as an unnecessary concern? They could, except for one problem. Their Master didn't.
> **—Max Lucado**

Act like Acts

Read Acts 6:1–7.

■ The Jerusalem church was already doing a good amount to help Jewish widows, but the non-Jews were being overlooked. Today, make a phone call or send an e-mail to someone who is knowledgeable about the needs in your community. Ask this simple question: Who are the three most overlooked groups of people in our community?

A Life Outlived

■ The Bible is filled with examples of how the poor were Jesus' priority. He never turned down an opportunity to listen and care for those in need. In what ways are you making the poor your priority? What are your best efforts so far, and what are the brightest ideas you have about meeting the needs of the neglected? Be specific!

❧ Day 5: With Him

When people create a resume, they usually brag on their accomplishments. Every previous position is described with indispensible terms. Each degree sounds impressive. All the references are glowing. Instead of being unemployed for a few years, they label their occupation during that time as "independent contractor" or "freelancer," or, even better, "consultant." They might not lie, but they definitely cast things in as positive a light as possible. This is the nature of resume-writing.

The apostles often had this kind of attitude, even arguing about who would get to sit at the right and left hand of Jesus in the new government they assumed he would launch. But none of their accomplishments or experiences was the focus of the Sanhedrin as they leveled accusations toward the apostles in Acts 4. Instead, they took note that Peter and John were "unschooled, ordinary men." What's more, they "took note that these men had been with Jesus" (Acts 4:13 NIV). In matters of faith, no qualification or experience is more important than simply being with your Savior.

Act like Acts

Read Acts 4:8–13.

■ You may worry that you don't have enough education, talent, time, or money to make a difference, but the disciples didn't have those things either. They just took advantage of the opportunity God gave them. Imagine what opportunities are right in front of you this week. How can you share your faith or help those in need? Seize those moments before they pass.

A Life Outlived

■ Are you overwhelmed with the tasks of helping those in need? Do you lack courage to speak the truth of the gospel? The best way to gain the power needed to speak and serve in these situations is to spend time with Jesus. What are your daily, weekly, and monthly routines for spending meaningful time with God? How can you adjust those habits to ensure you are the kind of person people will notice has "been with Jesus" as the disciples were?

Legacy Starter:
Higher Calling Auction

You expect to hear a familiar preaching tone from the pulpit of a church, not the high-speed negotiating of an auctioneer. But on a Friday night at a church in Spring Lake, Michigan, it was an auctioneer rattling off numbers, not a preacher rattling off verses.[6] After becoming more aware of the great need for clean water in Haiti and El Salvador, this church body was determined to get the word out and raise money to dig and repair wells. Their idea: a Heart for the World Auction.

They got people in the church to donate high-quality items, everything from baskets of goodies to tickets for sports events and concerts. The lobby was outfitted with tables displaying everything for the silent auction, and the sanctuary became the auction house for the more expensive items. A speaker from a world relief organization got them all pumped up and then everything was auctioned off. When all was said and done, they had raised $26,000 to meet the clean-water needs of those communities.

Could your church do something like this? You could do a large-scale church auction similar to this one or a smaller-scale yard sale with the same objectives. Here are a few suggestions to help you get started:

Large-Scale Church Auction

This auction event can be held to raise awareness for global relief needs and other concerns within the church and your entire community or to raise funds for a specific humanitarian project. The scale of this kind of event would require all the leadership of your church, particularly your missions committee and your pastor, to be on board.

You would also need start-up funds for the event in order to promote it as well as hiring an auctioneer, speaker, band, and so on. The other reason for having start-up funds is that you don't want the auction donations to merely cover the expenses. Ideally, all the money given would go to the humanitarian project directly.

A key to success with this kind of event is the donation of quality items for auction and the communication of the event night. Plan it out way in advance, and if you do, it can be a remarkably effective and interesting way to focus on the have-nots around the world.

Smaller-Scale Church Yard Sale

If the auction is too much for your church to bite off this year, look into budgeting for it in the future. Instead do a smaller-scale, cheaper church yard sale. You will want to approach the yard sale the same way as the auction in order to raise both awareness and funds for a humanitarian project. However, allow people to donate used items that can be priced and sold as you would for a neighborhood yard sale. A yard sale of this nature could be a great way for you to get started in involving lots of people in changing the world.

✿ Group Discussion

There are those who have and those who have not. The rich become richer, it seems, and the poor, poorer. It doesn't seem right to have so few with so much and so many with so little. The disciple Judas, who had been dipping into the fund for the poor, grumbled that money was being wasted on Jesus. The Savior replied, "You have the poor with you always" (Matthew 26:11). Some quote this verse to defend the idea that tackling issues of poverty is useless, but we are reminded that the Bible is full of hundreds upon hundreds of verses challenging us to respond to the poor.

And of course part of the problem is that the poor are so often *not* with us. They are segregated and contained in places where don't see them. You have to cross to the other side of the tracks. You have to fly over oceans. They are in another country. Another neighborhood. In a place where the haves don't see the have-nots.

We can ask ourselves two questions in response. First, why do so many not have what we have? This question is difficult. The answer is even more challenging and complex than we can imagine. Poverty is not a simple problem, and no simple solutions have shown themselves. But the more pressing question than "why?" is "what?" That is, what are we to do about it? What is our responsibility in the face of ever-present poverty in the world? What should the haves do for the have-nots?

1. Before you watch the video, each person in the group should spend a moment describing the worst situation of poverty they have ever witnessed. Was it on a special trip? Was it recent or long ago? How did it affect your view of those who do without so much?

2. After you watch the video, discuss the following questions:
   a. In three sub-groups, look up the following verses on how we should place a priority on the poor. Report back to the entire group with what you find.

Group 1	Group 2	Group 3
Psalm 140:12	Isaiah 41:17	Luke 6:20–21
James 2:5	Jeremiah 22:3	Isaiah 58:6
Proverbs 22:9	Luke 3:11	Proverbs 19:17
Isaiah 10:1–3	Proverbs 29:7	Luke 6:24

b. What specific ministries for the homeless exist in your community? Who do you know who already volunteers in them? What does the homeless problem look like in your area or in the nearest large city? How could your group and your church become more active in addressing this need?

c. Jonathan's small group is making a difference in their local community. As a group, make a list of at least ten wild ideas for a local project, like the "Laundry Love People" project, that your group could do together in your community. What are the two or three ideas that you could try to accomplish in the next few months, and which one are you going to do first?

d. How do the problems of modern-day slavery and sex trafficking stir your spirit? How might those who opposed racial slavery in America and Europe feel toward modern-day slavery?

e. What do you think you'd do if you found yourself unexpectedly in the middle of a crisis, as Ben and Katie were after Haiti's earthquake? Describe how overwhelming that experience would be for you. Would you rise to the challenge as they did? What skills and passions would suddenly become useful?

f. In Luke 4:14–21 we have what almost sounds like a mission statement from Jesus, read in his hometown of Nazareth. How does his message and mission sound to people today? What if he showed up and said similar things in your church or your city? What would be the response? What was the eventual response of those in Nazareth to Jesus in Luke 4:28–30?

g. In Acts 6 the church of Jerusalem had a problem related to the poor in their community, specifically the widows who didn't have enough food. To address the problem, they did two things: 1) they all got involved; and 2) they selected some of the best among them to lead the solution. Discuss those two areas in your context. What are the easiest and most accessible ways for your entire church to be more involved in addressing the needs of the poor? Who are the best and brightest people or organizations in your church, in your community, and around the world who address these issues?

3. Take time as a group to pray for the people and organizations you listed in the previous question. Ask God to bless them and inspire your support of them.

"Pure and genuine religion in the sight
of God the Father means caring for
orphans and widows in their distress and
refusing to let the world corrupt you."

(James 1:27 NLT)

Dear Lord, you've commanded me to search my heart,
and I humbly ask you to give me wisdom as I look at the
person you've made me to be. Show me my strengths,
and give me creative ideas on how I can use those gifts
for your glory. Help me to make a difference in times of
crisis and times of peace, that through my actions others
may know of your goodness. In Jesus' name, amen.

WEEK

BREAKING
DOWN
WALLS

In Christ's family there can be no
division into Jew and non-Jew,
slave and free, male and female.
Among us you are all equal.
That is, we are all in a common
relationship with Jesus Christ.

(Galatians 3:28 MSG)

✿ Day 1: Unintentional Missionaries

From the start it was supposed to spread. If Jesus ended his ministry in New York City, he would have sent them to New Jersey, the East Coast, and anywhere planes from the international airport could reach. If the ascension had happened in China, it would be Beijing first, then Japan, Australia, and anywhere boats could reach. But because he was in Jerusalem, Jesus said the disciples would be his witnesses far beyond that holy city to Judea (the surrounding area), to Samaria (the neighboring state), and to the very ends of the earth (Acts 1:8).

The early church seemed to have been quite comfortable staying in Jerusalem at first; by Acts 8, we see that the gospel had not traveled very far. But then everything changed: widespread persecution of Christians began after the stoning of Stephen. While it was the worst of times for many in Jerusalem who followed Christ, it was also the best of times for the Christian faith, as the gospel traveled with the fleeing Christians. They became unintentional missionaries because of their difficult circumstances.

Act like Acts

Read Acts 8:1–8 and then skim over the next few chapters of Acts.
◼ Although the church was scattered by persecution, it also sparked a season of growth and rise in the early Christian faith. How might God want the difficulties to be opportunities to love others and share your faith across the dividing walls? Even though you may not have planned

it, you can start today to make the most of these opportunities to reach out and break down walls.

A Life Outlived

■ If we're honest about it, we all have walls that keep someone out. In what areas of your life do you find yourself clearly on one side while people you've come to frown upon, even disdain, stand on the other? Make a list here of the walls that bisect your world. How can you start to break down these walls starting today?

Get Unshelled:
Identifying Walls

Have you ever walked through a house or building while it's being built? When the contractors begin framing the house, it's fun to imagine the rooms and windows that will soon appear. As you start to see how the house will be laid out, you begin to picture how a family will make the house their home. When the walls go up, the space is defined.

Our desire for definition is part of why we build figurative walls around ourselves too. Those mental walls between yourself and another person define you. As a result, tearing down walls that stand between you and other people can be a very worrying process. All change is hard—and change that threatens who you've perceived yourself to be is the hardest kind of change. But the walls between you and people (or people groups) who are different than you must come down if you are to fully experience who God wants you to be.

Reflect on the following questions to help you restate your identity in Christ so that this change is easier to complete:

■ *Your Father in Heaven.* Jesus taught us to start our prayers by saying, "Our Father in heaven." How does it help to think of yourself as a child of God? Why that is important to your identity?

■ *Relationships that Define You.* Part of the core of your identity is your relationship to others. If you're married, you are a husband or a wife. If you have a job, you're an employee. A brother might have a sister and the other way around. Relationships make us parents and children, students and teachers, neighbors and friends. List here the most important relationships in your life and how they shape your identity.

■ *Dividing Walls.* Reflect here on the walls that have divided you from other kinds of people in the past. Consider these categories and write down what types of people you have held at a distance or had difficulty showing the love of Christ toward. Pray for God to give you the grace to overcome these walls, tearing them down as Jesus would.

☀ Day 2: Any Reason Not To?

As part of the scattering of the believers, Philip, one of the early leaders of the church, left Jerusalem to spread the gospel. He came across a man from Ethiopia, the eunuch of Acts 8. Consider the many differences between the two:

	Philip	The Ethiopian
Skin:	Light	Dark
Home:	Greek Empire	Africa
Class:	Poor refugee	Rich traveler
Family:	Father of four	None (he was a eunuch)

When you think about it, part of this conversation's marvel was how different the two men were from one another. Philip crossed these walls that separated them and made a difference in the eunuch's life, and for the first time the faith left the Middle East, gaining an influential convert on the continent of Africa.

> The cross of Christ creates a new people, a people unhindered by skin color or family feud. A new citizenry based, not on common ancestry or geography, but on a common Savior.
> **—Max Lucado**

Act like Acts

Read Acts 8:26–40.

Notice how Philip was prompted by God merely to stay near the Ethiopian. God didn't tell him what to say or how to say it. Who has God been prompting you to connect with lately? Is there someone in your life with whom you might need to go out of your way to relate to? Make it your mission to do so and see what happens. Pray about it, and opportunities will present themselves.

A Life Outlived

■ Philip walked in a world where many things were reserved for the few. Even the Jewish religion was reserved for a specific ethnicity (or for those who wanted to join and submit fully to that culture). But, given an opportunity to extend friendship, grace, and the gospel—Philip took it. Do you have interactions with anyone who is as different from you as the Ethiopian eunuch was from Philip? What are the reasons that person can "have what you have"? Can you become a part of the solution like Philip was?

☀ Day 3: Anyone but That Guy

Could there have been anyone worse for God to tell Ananias to visit? Saul was someone to avoid, not to seek out. As a leader in the Christian church, Ananias was a prime target for serial-persecutor Saul. This man had papers from the high court to arrest any Christians he found in Damascus, and those arrested were often stoned to death, as Stephen had been. Yet God asked Ananias to go to Saul and help him. Jesus had a plan for Saul, he was told.

God had chosen this Saul to be the apostle to the Gentiles, to carry the gospel to the heart of the Roman world. At first, Ananias could not believe it. *Anyone but that guy*, he must have thought. Saul was the last person Ananias wanted to see, but Ananias was clearly commanded to go to him. So he did.

Act like Acts

Read Acts 9:1–19.

■ You could find no one in first-century Jerusalem who would have been more unlikely to convert to Christianity than Saul. Yet God found a way to shock him into reality and to not only convert him but also commission him to the cause of reaching the Gentiles. Spend time in prayer today for someone who is very far from God, someone you might even be afraid of or fear because they seem to be an enemy of God. Ask God to confront that person and change his or her heart.

A Life Outlived

■ We often forget that God uses ordinary people to reach others who will be used extraordinarily. You might only need to witness to one person, and that person could in turn influence an entire people group. Paul had a massive impact in the world, but don't forget Ananias, the man who led Paul to Christ. Has God given you a similar mission? Is there a Saul in your life?

A Mile in Their Shoes:
Homeless Walk

More than 2 million people are homeless in any given year in the United States. Some estimates put the number at more than 3 million.[7] How about walking a mile in their shoes, literally? You can organize a community-wide walk of solidarity with those who are homeless, or engage in a smaller-scale homeless walk on your own to pray for the homeless and increase your awareness of their needs.

Community Homeless Walk

A community-wide homeless walk is generally large scale and often includes a walk through the poorer sections of the city to increase awareness. The local media tends to cover the event. If you feel called to do this, spend some time discovering whether your community already has a walk planned. Your local community foundation or rescue mission would be a good place to ask. If a homeless walk is scheduled, sign up or register to take part. To make this kind of walk more meaningful, you can do any number of the following:

☐ *Get per-mile sponsors.* Donate the money your sponsors pledge in your name to a local homeless shelter or group that works with the homeless.

☐ *Include the homeless in your walk.* Ask the local homeless shelter if those staying in that temporary housing could be involved. Or at the minimum, plan for a way to bless the homeless you see along the way through encouragement, a prayer, or a meal card.

☐ *Pray for the homeless.* Use this walk as a time of more-intense intercession for the poor and homeless in your area. Allow this activity and prayer time to work on your heart.

☐ *Talk about it.* Relate the experience to others and tell them they should join you next year. Report back to your small group and church on the event.

Personal Homeless Walk

In communities without a larger homeless walk to join, you can engage in a similar meaningful experience with your family or group. Schedule a date to do a prayer walk in the nearest inner city to your town; you may need to travel to a larger city nearby. Make sure everyone has a street map of the area. Mark out routes for groups of three or four (do not go alone) to walk and pray. Encourage your group to pray out loud (with their eyes open so they can keep walking) for the needs of the poor and homeless in that area. Pray for whatever you see along the way that sparks your imagination or grips your heart with compassion. Meet back at one place to debrief the time and pray as a family or group.

⚜ **Day 4:** Unclean

From the time he was a small child, Peter was taught what was good and bad, right and wrong, clean and unclean. On the unclean list were things not to do, places not to go, and food not to eat. The eating habits in particular set apart a Jew like Peter. What you did not eat was crucial. Pork, shellfish, and reptiles, for example, were on the "not" list. But just as important as what you didn't eat was *who* you didn't eat *with*. Namely: Gentiles.

This problem was crucial for the early church, as Jesus had made it clear that the gospel message would spread around the world. But how could the Jews, who were set apart, have fellowship with Gentiles if they couldn't even eat together? The Lord's Supper itself would have to be segregated. While the laws and regulations for eating set the Jews apart for a time, the solution to sin had come: salvation through the Savior, Jesus Christ. So the rules had changed. Peter's experience in Acts 10 made that clear. God was providing a way for Gentiles and Jews to not only receive forgiveness, but also to be reconciled with each other in unity.

> Jesus was more concerned about bringing everyone in than shutting certain people out. This was the tension Peter felt. His culture said, "Keep your distance from Gentiles." His Christ said, "Build bridges to Gentiles." And Peter had to make a choice.
>
> **—Max Lucado**

Act like Acts

Read Acts 10:1–48 as well as Acts 11:1–18.

▪ Make a list of all the cultural biases between the Jews and the Gentiles mentioned in this passage. When have you been in an environment that was out of your comfort zone or diverse enough that you began to notice your own cultural biases? How did you react?

A Life Outlived

▪ Our cultural context and family upbringing is hard to break. We are taught from our youth that certain people are on the opposite side of the wall from us. How have you been influenced by parents, friends, teachers, or other people during your upbringing to distrust or avoid certain people? Ask for God to work in your heart about these prejudices and give yourself opportunities to confirm the change in your heart.

⚘ **Day 5:** Be a Barnabas

Barnabas was a good man. That's what Acts 11:24 tells us. He did many good things, from giving money to the church to encouraging the new believers in Antioch. He is most notable for traveling with Paul throughout the Roman world, converting Gentiles and establishing churches. In fact, we can see a marked change in Barnabas throughout Acts, which mentions the man twenty-three times. At the beginning we observe Barnabas acting alone. Then we see Barnabas advocating for Paul (formerly Saul) to ensure he has a place of ministry. Finally, from Acts 13 on, it is nearly always "Paul and Barnabas." He's listed second, no doubt an afterthought to Paul for some.

Have you ever felt that way? That you played second fiddle? Been the backup role? Slipped into the shadows behind someone else? It can be a difficult position. However, we never see this encouraging "good man" named Barnabas struggle with it. Some people have amazing gifts like Paul. They're *great*. But God uses ordinary people like Barnabas too, who are simply *good*.

Act like Acts

Read Acts 4:36–37 and Acts 11:19–30.

■ Barnabas always brings encouragement with him. He encourages the church in Jerusalem with his sizeable gift. Then he is given a special name meaning "son of encouragement." He encourages the church in Antioch as God does something special among them. Then he goes looking for Paul and encourages him to come from Tarsus to Antioch.

Take the time to be a Barnabas today and write three encouraging notes to people you know who need it. To whom will you write?

A Life Outlived

■ In Acts 13:1–3 we read about a group of leaders in Antioch of which Barnabas was a part. The group included those from different economic and religious backgrounds, several nationalities (African, Syrian, Cyprian, and Palestinian), and a variety of skin colors. How can you, like Barnabas, support the leadership of someone you know who is different from you?

Legacy Starter:
The Most Segregated Hour of the Week

Many people have observed that the most segregated hour of the week in America is Sunday morning worship. No matter how hard they may try, most churches are not multiethnic. It can take many, many years for a church to become more diverse in leadership and attendance. And that transition is dependent on so many factors that may not be in your control.

However, having positive relationships with churches of other ethnicities can be a first step toward breaking down walls. In fact, you may find that a church predominantly made up of people different than you is thinking the same things, and building a relationship would help them in their single-ethnicity limitations too. Here are a few possibilities for building a positive partnership with the people in a church that looks different than yours:

- [ ] *Eat together*. There's nothing quite as good as a church potluck—unless you make that a two-church potluck. Instead of just doing a carry-in dinner alone, consider combining this low-key time of fellowship with another church, Sunday school class, or small group that is different than your own. Getting a bit tired of Sister Mable's seven-layer salad? Think of all the new food you'll get to try at this pitch-in.

- [ ] *Serve together*. When coordinating a service project, call up another church and see whether they'd like to join you. Team up for a more effective time of service and new diverse relationships too.

- [ ] *Pray together*. Connect with inter-racial and inter-denominational prayer times, or just combine prayer meetings with another church for a week. It's really hard to turn down an offer to pray with someone.

- [ ] *Worship together*. Instead of doing your special service alone, partner with another church to pull it off. Sometimes these special services, such as a Thanksgiving Eve, Good Friday, or holiday events, have smaller attendance anyway and it would be the perfect time to share a sanctuary and a pew with someone different than you.

☐ *Share pastors.* A "pulpit swap" can be a great way for two pastors to bless each other's congregation and give them a taste of another style of preaching.

☐ *Share resources.* Your church may have something others don't and vice versa. It can be as small as sharing group study materials (like this one) or as large as sharing a church bus. Some churches even have multiple congregations of different ethnicities or languages meeting in the same building.

✿ **Group** Discussion

The walls that divide us are sometimes obvious, while other times they are invisible but just as real. Our neighborhoods tend to be comprised of people from just one socio-economic level. One community is home to half-million-dollar houses, while another fifteen minutes away might be full of condemned and decrepit buildings where squatters live. One block is predominately Hispanic, the next Caucasian, and the one after that, African-American. Individuals with elite jobs don't associate with people who punch the clock. You're on this side of a wall, and they are on the other.

You didn't build the wall, that's for sure. It was there long before you came around. Walls are a part of life. We're all different. We have different appearances, different incomes, difference cultures, different values, and different opportunities. These differences begin to build up walls—barriers that are sometimes hard to bridge, in either direction.

The walls that divide us often seem so high and so thick that nothing can blast through them. But Jesus and the early church broke down walls on a routine basis. Gender walls crumbled. Jews ate with Gentiles. Rich and poor worshiped together. Dark-skinned people taught light-skinned people, and vice versa. Slaves and free both experienced the true liberty of Christian community.

How can we break down our walls? We can start by making unity the core of our mission, just as it was for the early church.

1. Before you watch the video, spend some time as a group looking at a map of your area. What barriers divide different groups? Who tends to live where? What kinds of people gather in certain neighborhoods? Mark the map to show where the walls are found, including both visible and invisible walls. What is happening already, and what should happen to break down walls?

2. After you watch the video, discuss the following questions:

a. How does the story of Ron and his teen daughters in the park inspire you? What places do you go where people different from you also hang out?

b. Which phrase or quote from the video today would you put on a bumper sticker or use as a slogan for your life?

c. Read Galatians 3:26–29 together as a group. According to verse 26, what causes us to be sons and daughters of God? How do you think the word picture in verse 27 of being clothed with Christ could ensure there are no walls between "Jew nor Greek, slave nor free, male nor female"?

d. What are some things people say that are insensitive to others who are different from them? What do you think of being "politically correct"? When have you noticed a person trying to speak the truth but failing to do so in love (Ephesians 4:15)?

e. What could you do to cheer for those on the other side of
   the wall, like those at the football game in Grapevine, Texas?
   What small but significant things did they do to make sure the
   convicted criminals on the other team knew they were cared for?

f. The players and fans at the school in Grapevine, Texas, did not
   physically change the situation for those convicted criminals.
   The prisoners went back under lock and key that very night. But
   despite this, what impact did it have on the students?

3. Spend time as a group making a list of people who are different from you for whom you could be praying. Pray for them as groups or as individuals by name—asking God to give you the opportunity to break down dividing walls.

> Therefore, accept each other just
> as Christ has accepted you so
> that God will be given glory.
>
> (Romans 15:7 NLT)

Heavenly Father, I've built walls around me so that I might have a more comfortable life, but those walls reveal prejudices I've hidden deep down within me. Tear those walls down, so that I may serve others in love. Bring people into my community and into my life who I may, previously, have avoided. Teach me more about you. Show me how to love in a way I never expected to. In Jesus' name, amen.

WEEK

FOR ALL
THE RIGHT
REASONS

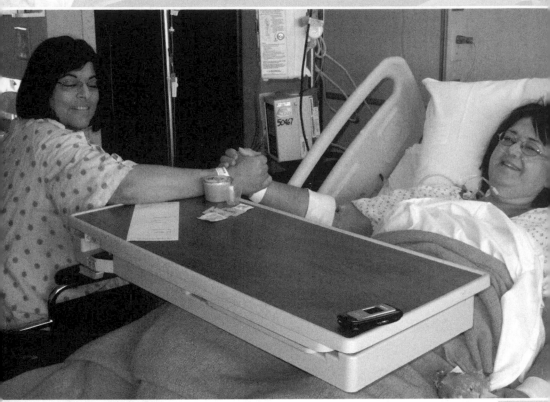

"When you give to someone in
need, don't tell your left hand
what your right hand is doing."

(Matthew 6:3 NLT)

❧ Day 1: I'm Kind of a Big Deal

Simon the Sorcerer, whom we meet in Acts 8, was the kind of guy who would have worn a shirt with "I'm kind of a big deal" on it, but with no irony intended. He thought he was big stuff. We see Simon astonishing the crowds with his magic tricks and giving speeches "claiming that he was someone great" (Acts 8:9). His own greatest fan and personal publicist, Simon was quite full of himself.

When Peter and John came to town, Simon's pride reared its ugly head. The disciples laid hands on people and prayed that they would receive the Holy Spirit. Once Simon saw the wonderful filling of the Spirit, his first thought wasn't his own infilling or even how this would be good for the church. Instead, he saw it as yet another trick he could learn to boost his magic show, making himself appear even greater. He had the gall to offer money to Peter and John so they would give him this power.

You can imagine what happened next. Peter and John confronted Simon the Sorcerer, saying that the Holy Spirit is not for sale. Not only that, but they pointed out Simon's sinful pride. He had to watch his mouth and check his attitude. He thought he was a big deal, but he learned that, among believers, the only big deal is God.

Act like Acts

Read Acts 8:9–25.

■ What was Simon the Sorcerer's motivation for wanting to gain the Holy Spirit's power? How are you tempted to be prideful? Intentionally deflect any praise or thanks you receive today, giving the glory to God and thanks to others. When something goes well, don't seek credit. When you deserve to be thanked, don't grow to expect it. Don't dwell on "getting what's yours." Instead, give it away.

A Life Outlived

■ The falseness of hypocrisy rankles God. It is sin, and God takes it very seriously. Are you sure you're being the real you around people in your family? at work? at church? How do you know?

Get Unshelled:
Credit Chart

While pride is a private sin, public recognition for our "good deeds" is so often the desire of a prideful heart. We don't say we want the credit, but it sure feels great when we receive it. We finally get the attention we were looking for. All the work and sacrifice becomes worth it. Or is it? Is that why we do the good we do?

It can be very difficult to figure out your motives for doing good works. Sometimes they aren't exposed until the moment when you don't get credit for something, and you try to make sure others notice it. Or at other times when you do receive credit, you savor the compliments, stopping too long to enjoy the praise.

Below you'll find a Credit Chart to help you process certain situations when you've done something good and received credit for it. This chart can help you think about how you can share credit with God and others and how you might do the same thing without drawing notice the next time, working harder to do good for all the right reasons.

A Good Thing I Did:	Credit Already Received:	How I Could Share the Credit:	How I Could Do This Quietly:
Example 1: Bought the perfect present for office staff to give boss for Boss's Day	Told the boss I bought it, and she thanked me in the meeting	Personally thank each person who chipped in for the gift	Don't emphasize that I shopped for the gift and give it in secret next time
Example 2: Gave a lot of money to a missionary at church	He thanked me in front of the whole church as being one of his key supporters	Ensure that gift is seen as from our entire family, not just me	Next time I'll send the check in to the home office instead of giving it to him in person

✿ **Day 2:** Are You a Dorcas?

Are you a Dorcas? No, it's not an insult. Dorcas was a wonderful lady in Acts who lived so well for God that she got to live twice. That's right. She lived, died, and then lived again. Dorcas is described as someone who "was always doing good and helping the poor" (Acts 9:36 NIV). Her reputation extended all the way to the traveling Peter, who rushed to her bedside when he heard she had become sick and died. He sent everyone out of the room and then spoke to the servant-minded Dorcas as if she were alive, telling her to "get up." She did.

So, the first person to rise from the dead after Jesus was a woman known for her modest service of the poor, someone who was always doing good works. Doesn't that seem to be the exact description of someone to whom God would give a second chance at life?

> Jesus will recount, one by one,
> all our acts of kindness. The works
> of mercy are simple deeds. And
> yet, in these simple deeds we serve
> Jesus. Astounding this truth: we serve
> Christ by serving needy people.
> **—Max Lucado**

Act like Acts

Read Acts 9:26–43.

■ How would you live differently if you came back to life after dying? What new perspective would this experience bring? How would your conversations be different? How would your priorities shift? Do you have any good reasons for not making these shifts now?

A Life Outlived

No one can do it all on his own, but we can all help in some way. Even if you just make an impact on one life, you're serving Jesus. And that changed life may go on to impact others and the ripple effect starts. So if you're ever overwhelmed with the task of helping so many in need, start with doing just one thing for one person today. As you serve, remember that you are serving Jesus, not looking for credit or reward or even to be noticed at all. How could you serve someone today without others knowing?

Day 3: House-to-House

If you went looking for the early Christians, the best place to find them going about their ministry was a house. The word for *house* is used twenty-six times in Acts alone. And the community life of the early church is often characterized as happening from "house to house." Healings, preaching, conversions, baptisms, and worship—all these things took place in or near households. One of the greatest tools God used to spread the gospel was the house.

Does he still use houses to do his work? Think of someone you know who hosts a small group Bible study in his home. Recall that neighbor who uses her gift of hospitality to have people over all the time. Think of the couple who invites new people over each week after church. Surely the gospel is still spreading house to house. Is it spreading from your home?

Act like Acts

Read Acts 2:46 and Acts 5:42.

◼ How have other people used their homes to be welcoming to you? When have you benefitted from the hospitality of others? What would your life look like if you spent more time with people in your living room or theirs?

A Life Outlived

◼ There are plenty of reasons we come up with that stand in the way of reaching out. There is no need to procrastinate. Profound things can happen when we have the courage to open our hearts and homes—right now, just the way they are. Who can you invite over to your home this week? Connect with them to put it on the schedule or spontaneously just invite them over tonight.

A Mile in Their Shoes:
Undercover Servant

Every day people work in service industries or other low-income jobs; they are often called "the working poor." These jobs are usually minimum wage. Because they are offered at part-time with no benefits, a person usually has to work two or three of them in order to pay the bills.

Sometime in the next week and a few times this month, take on one of these jobs for free for a few hours. If possible, do it in secret so no one will find out. This activity is to help you walk a mile in someone else's shoes, not to get credit for your service. Choose from one of the many examples below or seek out another option not listed:

☐ *Bathroom Cleanup.* Next Sunday, serve in a way that no one will see but will make a big difference: stay after church and clean the bathrooms. Bring a bucket of equipment and supplies to help you do the job or find the place where such things are stored at the church.

☐ *Do Not Disturb.* Next time you stay in a hotel, clean it up before you leave. Do anything you can to make the housekeeping staff's job easier—pull the sheets and towels and stack them by the door, tie up the bags of trash and leave them in an easy place to be removed. By taking fifteen to twenty minutes to do this, you're saving a hard-working housekeeper some precious time as well.

☐ *Lawn Mowing*. The next time your neighbors are away on vacation, mow their lawn and never tell them who did it. If you live in a snowy area, shovel off their driveway and sidewalk for them while they're away or at work.

☐ *Dish Duty*. Volunteer at a local soup kitchen or other meal to be the dishwasher. This hidden and thankless job is hard and messy. Come ready to get a bit sloppy.

☐ *Garbage Collection*. Take trash bags to a local park or the side of a local highway and collect trash. This job is one even minimum-wage employees don't want to do; prisoner work details are often assigned to this task.

■ Whichever option you choose, spend time reflecting on what this service felt like for you to do. Was it humbling? Was it frustrating? Was it hard? Would you do it for the amount of money usually paid for these jobs? Consider how hard it would be to live off that income and to do that work repeatedly. How does this experience affect your view of the working poor today?

✿ **Day 4:** Praise Grenades

We know it is bad form to do or say something so that someone else will praise us. The "look at me" approach doesn't garner as much praise as we would like. But we still remain prideful—we want to do good works, loudly, so they might be seen and we could get our "good ol' boy" and corresponding pat on the head.

So we devise a different strategy than the direct approach. We do something good and we do it quietly, but we ensure that in some way it will be traced back to us. We accidentally put our name on it. We leave the price tag on the gift intentionally. We tell just one person who we know will pass it on. We do our good works but we toss out praise grenades that are timed to go off shortly after we leave. When people explode into praise of our good deeds, we demure with false humility, all the while pleased that we were found out. Little did they know that we set the timer on the praise precisely for that moment.

No one knows what we're doing when we use praise grenades; we trick everyone with our compliment time bombs. Everyone but God, that is. He knows everything. And he takes this backhanded pride very seriously. Just look at what happened to Ananias and Sapphira in Acts 5. The consequences of using our good works for personal gain can be serious, so we shouldn't pull the pin on our praise grenades anymore. One just might go off in our hands next time.

People talk to us as if we are something special. Feels nice. Kudos become ladder rungs, and we begin to elevate ourselves. We shed our smallness, discard the Clark Kent glasses, and don a Superman swagger. We forget. We forget who brought us here. . . . Take time to remember. Remember who held you in the beginning. Remember who holds you today.

—Max Lucado

Act like Acts

Read Acts 4:36–37 and Acts 5:1–11.

■ How would you compare and contrast the way Barnabas and Ananias gave? What was similar? What were the key differences? Do you have any extra income or unexpected money that has come your way? Consider following the example of Barnabas and giving the total sum away as a blessing to others. However, be absolutely sure you are not doing it to seek credit or to manipulate the gift in order to be praised, like Ananias and Sapphira did.

A Life Outlived

■ Do you have spiritual habits or use some words in your speech that draw undue attention to yourself? Do you sit in front so everyone can see you're there? Do you sing like you're trying to get a record deal? Do you raise your hands in praise or in pride? Do you have a tendency to intentionally lob praise grenades out there where you hope the credit comes back to you? How could you eliminate these from your life?

❧ Day 5: Secret Service

After we've humbled ourselves and trained our minds and hearts to do good works for God's glory alone, the game changes entirely. Like secret agents, we go about our tasks intentionally concealing ourselves. We operate like the secret service agents who guard the president of the United States; no one notices us. And when someone does praise you, you use it as an opportunity to pass the praise to others and the glory to God.

The root of the matter is not the specific ways we conceal our good works or how we do things to be praised. It's a heart issue at its core. If in your heart you want praise, you will find a way to get it. If in your heart you are submitted to God fully and are not seeking praise, then you'll find a way to avoid reward on earth in favor of reward in heaven.

So start with the core question: why? Ask yourself *why* you're doing something. When you find your conscience challenging you on an action or you find yourself wondering if you're doing it for the right reasons, pause and ask yourself why you are doing it. This isn't an excuse to not do good deeds or give to others. Instead, by firmly confirming in your spirit that you do not want the credit, you become empowered for truly secret service. "Then your Father, who sees what is done in secret, will reward you" (Matthew 6:4 NIV).

Act like Acts

Read Matthew 6:1–8, 19–24.

■ What might the rewards of righteousness be in heaven? Can you imagine how God might like to reward you then? It seems that it is okay, even desired by God, for you to have treasures in heaven. Consider now how much more meager any reward or credit you might get on earth would compare to what you might receive in heaven. Reflect on this when giving your time, talent, and resources to the church and to those in need.

A Life Outlived

■ Giving charitably is about more than just the tax credit; we so often want the social and spiritual credit too. We want to get credit for being good people when we give. As Jesus said in Matthew 6:3, "When you give to someone in need, don't let your left hand know what you right hand is doing (NLT). How can you ensure your financial giving is done in secret? Are you already seen as a giver? If so, how could you be quieter about it in the future? Do you plan to give more in the coming days than you did in the past? How could you ensure your giving is unseen?

Legacy Starter:
Recurring Open House

It can be difficult these days to connect with your neighbors. In the suburbs, everyone seems to pull up into their garages and shut the door before anyone gets the chance to talk to one another. And when people do go outside, it's to their *back*yard. In the city, the mass of humanity marches in and out of subways without a word—and then hides away in their apartments behind a half dozen locks. Our culture isn't one that fosters community very well. What can you do about it?

Try opening your doors to your neighbors on a routine basis. Make it a low-key option—something for which they don't have to get all dressed up to impress. Try these ideas out to see whether they work for you and your neighbors.

☐ *Soup Night.* Warm up a Crock-Pot of soup and invite others to come over for a simple get-together on a certain night each week. If others ask if they can bring anything, tell them to bring a pot of soup and more neighbors. The idea is just to get together, not to impress anyone with your culinary arts—that level of having to perform becomes too hard to sustain over time.

☐ *Front-Porch Makeover.* Make your front porch a place where people want to hang out. Brew iced-tea or make lemonade and invite neighbors to stop over on Saturday or Sunday afternoons.

☐ *Open Game Night*. Put out all your board games on a certain night of the week and invite others to bring their own favorites, including kids games, and have a game night. Zero prep required.

☐ *Leftovers Night*. By the weekend, everyone on the block is just eating up the leftovers anyway—why not bring them all in one place and get the microwave humming? The only rule: nobody is allowed to make anything new.

☐ *Monday Night Football*. Invite neighbors over to watch the football game or another athletic event on a routine basis.

☐ *Facebook Group*. Start a Facebook group online and ask your neighbors to join. You may get to know them better online than you have so far chatting in the street.

☐ *Block Party*. Schedule a once-a-month block party while the weather cooperates. Everyone brings a dish to share. This works great in a cul-de-sac or in front of an apartment building.

🐾 **Group** Discussion

Saying one thing, then doing another. That's hypocrisy, the great plague of the church. It's the virus of pride and deceit that most turns off the non-believer and most cripples the authenticity of the believer.

God takes many things seriously, but in the earliest Jerusalem church he appears to take this issue more seriously than anything else. Using the church as a way to gain personal advancement, to trumpet your good works, or to seek credit for the good you've done—these are the deadly sins of the early church. Have we forgotten to take these sins as seriously as our God takes them?

It's hard enough to do something good. You have to overcome your fears, muster up the courage, and then do something difficult or stretching. Doing good is often money-consuming and time-consuming. In the end, a small part of us, and sometimes a large part of us, begins to be prideful of our work. After all, we're the ones who did the good deed. And so the battle over doing good for the right reasons begins. It's hard enough to do something good; to do it in secret is even harder. But it proves the full authenticity of the act. A good deed done without others' knowledge is the ultimate test of a giving, caring, and loving spirit. How can we wage this final war on hypocrisy and serve in secret or give in private? What does it take to do good, and for all the right reasons?

1. Before you watch the video, discuss what kinds of hypocrisy have most affected people's views of the church. Why is hypocrisy the biggest complaint non-Christians have about Christians?

2. After you watch the video, discuss the following questions:

  a. What phrase or quote from the video most stood out to you? Which one do you think you'll remember the longest and why?

  b. Giving a kidney to a missionary is an inspiring but extreme example of how far Patricia was willing to go to do good for all the right reasons. Have you ever discovered a significant, selfless act that was done in secret? How are their actions and Patricia's good examples for you?

  c. Build a creative list of ways to keep your servanthood secret. What are the best ways to ensure you're doing good for all the right reasons?

d. How can you give generously to your church or to help others, and do so privately?

3. Reflect on how your group has been affected by this four-week *Outlive Your Life* study.

   a. How easy or hard is it for you to trust that God can use someone like you to make a difference?

   b. Go around the circle and let each person list one thing this study has caused them to think more deeply about and one thing they are going to do differently from now on.

"But when you give to the needy, do not let your left hand know what your right hand is doing, so that your giving may be in secret. Then your Father, who sees what is done in secret, will reward you."

(Matthew 6:3–4 NIV)

Father, as this study winds to a close, imprint the lessons I've learned deep in my heart that I may keep them with me as I go out into the world to serve others in your name. Reduce my desire for recognition and increase my passion for creatively making a difference in the world. May your Holy Spirit fill every ounce of my being, directing me in all my choices. In Jesus' name I pray, amen.

Endnotes

1. World Vision Inc., http://www.worldvisionacts.org/brokenbread/ (accessed March 12, 2010).

2. CIA World Factbook, www.cia.gov/library/publications/the-world-factbook/index.html (accessed April 12, 2010).

3. Statistics Canada, www40.statcan.gc.ca/l01/cst01/econ50-eng.htm, (accessed April 12, 2010).

4. U.S. Department of Commerce, Bureau of Economic Analysis, http://www.bea.gov/regional/gsp/ (accessed April 12, 2010).

5. Jean Ziegler, "The Right to Food: Report by the Special Rapporteur on the Right to Food, Mr. Jean Ziegler, Submitted in Accordance with Commission on Human Rights Resolution 2000/10." United Nations, p. 5, http://graduateinstitute.ch/faculty/clapham/hrdoc/docs/foodrep2001.pdf (accessed April 27, 2010).

6. Story used by permission from Dave Horne of Spring Lake Wesleyan Church and from their official press release dated January 6, 2010.

7. The Public Broadcasting System, http://www.pbs.org/now/shows/526/homeless-facts.html (accessed April 28, 2010).

SPECIAL THANKS

Host Todd Phillips is the pastor of the
3000-member Frontline Church in
Washington D.C. Todd is the author
of *Spiritual CPR* and *Get Uncomfortable*.
He speaks across the country at
conferences, including The RightNow
Conferences. Todd and his wife, Julie,
have three children.

More Resources
from Max Lucado

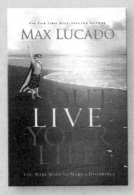

OUTLIVE YOUR LIFE

978-0-8499-2069-1, $24.99

These are difficult days in our world's history. 1.75 billion people are desperately poor, natural disasters are gouging entire nations, and economic uncertainty still reigns across the globe. But you and I have been given an opportunity to make a big difference. What if we did? What if we rocked the world with hope? Infiltrated all corners with God's love and life? We are created by a great God to do great works. He invites us to outlive our lives, not just in heaven, but here on earth. Let's live our lives in such a way that the world will be glad we did.

LIVE TO MAKE A DIFFERENCE

978-0-8499-4612-7, $2.99

Featuring key selections from *Outlive Your Life*, this booklet embodies the spirit of making a difference in the church as well as the local community, region, and world. Perfect for giving away to your church community, small group, or neighbors.

YOU CHANGED MY LIFE

978-1-4041-8783-2, $15.99

Sharing this inspiring message is the perfect way to thank teachers, pastors, and others who serve. This book also features a personal dedication page where givers celebrate the person who changed their lives.

ONE HAND, TWO HANDS

978-1-4003-1649-6, $16.99

With whimsical words and delightful illustrations, Max shows how even the youngest children can serve others and how little helping hands bring joy to those being served, to the child and to our heavenly Father!

Outlive Your Life Spanish Edition

978-1-6025-5404-7, $13.99

Outlive Your Life Audiobook

978-0-8499-4613-4, $24.99

Enjoy *Outlive Your Life* in Spanish or the unabridged audio.

The Lucado Life Lessons Study Bible

Hardcover
978-1-4185-4396-9, $49.99

Leathersoft black/gray
978-1-4185-4398-3, $69.99

Leathersoft burgundy/gray
978-1-4185-4399-0, $69.99

This beautifully designed Bible contains 1,000 practical application "Life Lessons" offering insights straight from Max Lucado's complete works including *Outlive Your Life*.

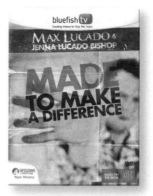

Made to Make a Difference Youth Curriculum

978-1-5727-5266-5, $99.99

BluefishTV presents this 4-session DVD series that follows the real-life stories of teens who are trying to make their lives count. With teaching by Max Lucado and hosted by Jenna Lucado, the study explores how the church in Acts left a legacy that students can continue to build upon 2,000 years later. Available at BluefishTV.com

You Were Made to Make a Difference Youth Book

978-1-4003-1600-7, $14.99

This adaptation of *Outlive Your Life* for teens offers practical tips youth can take into their community to make a difference, plus real-life stories about young people who have done just that.